IMAGES
of America

MEDORA AND THEODORE ROOSEVELT NATIONAL PARK

The relatively treeless plains of southwestern North Dakota were once covered with forests of hardwoods such as elm, hickory, and walnut, interspersed with conifers of gingkoes, figs, sequoia, and other trees. Some of these trees evidently grew large during climatic periods far different than present day. Four Medora area residents in early-20th-century western clothing admire a large upright petrified tree trunk that can still be seen by careful observers from the scenic loop road in the south unit of Theodore Roosevelt National Park. (Courtesy of Wally Owen, Indergaard family collection.)

On the Cover: The Rough Riders Hotel was named in honor of Theodore Roosevelt's Rough Riders of the Spanish-American War. The structure was originally named the Metropolitan Hotel by its owner George Fitzgerald. It has long been recognized as the visual and perhaps even the cultural center of Medora in the past. The hotel was reconstructed in the early 1960s by the Gold Seal Company of Bismarck. (Photograph by Doubleday-Myers; courtesy of Wally Owen, Indergaard family collection.)

IMAGES
of America

MEDORA AND THEODORE ROOSEVELT NATIONAL PARK

Gary Leppart

ARCADIA
PUBLISHING

Published by Arcadia Publishing
Charleston, South Carolina

Printed in the United States of America

Library of Congress Catalog Card Number: 2006940518

For all general information contact Arcadia Publishing at:
Telephone 843-853-2070
Fax 843-853-0044
E-mail sales@arcadiapublishing.com
For customer service and orders:
Toll-Free 1-888-313-2665

Visit us on the Internet at www.arcadiapublishing.com

This book is dedicated to my mother, Betty Cornell, and my late stepfather, Frederick Louis (Ted) Cornell. Ted was the Billings County sheriff for 30 years. He would have enjoyed this book. Also, for David, who would have been 60 years old in 2007.

CONTENTS

ACKNOWLEDGMENTS

I want to express my gratitude to Bruce Kaye, Theodore Roosevelt National Park chief of interpretation, for allowing me the liberal use of historic photographs in the park service collections at Medora. Without access to those collections, the photographs brought together for this publication would be far from complete.

I am also indebted to Doug Ellison, co-owner of the Western Edge Bookstore at Medora with his wife Mary, for recommending that I contact Arcadia Publishing regarding the publication of a historic photography book centered on my boyhood home of Medora and the nearby three units of Theodore Roosevelt National Park. You were right on target, Doug.

Diane Rogness, western regional manager for the State Historical Society of North Dakota at the Chateau de Mores provided very helpful information regarding various structures in Medora when I became stymied.

Diane, Doug, and Bruce reviewed draft manuscript copies prepared for this publication and offered helpful suggestions and alerted me to inaccuracies. Doug also provided images. Wally Owen of Medora very generously loaned me numerous historic photographs collected over many years by Duane Indergaard of Belfield, North Dakota. My mother, Betty Cornell, also provided a large number of images. Sydney Hegge of rural Medora provided images and clarifying information. My sister, Joanne Joyce of Medora, also provided details on features of the community as did Valerie Naylor, superintendent of Theodore Roosevelt National Park.

I also wish to thank the entire production staff of Arcadia Publishing for your support and creative skills applied to this book. I especially wish to thank Ann Marie Lonsdale, my editor, for her support and patience.

Thank you all very much.

INTRODUCTION

Two names that are synonymous with the early written history of the Little Missouri Badlands of southwestern North Dakota are the Marquis de Mores and Theodore Roosevelt. Both men arrived in the badlands in 1883: de Mores, in April, and Roosevelt a few months later in September. These individuals were to share a common interest in the potential for profit that was apparent in the grazing of cattle on the open ranges of western Dakota Territory.

The vast buffalo herds, or more correctly, bison herds which once roamed the northern Great Plains were all but gone by 1883. Individuals with vision such as de Mores and Roosevelt could easily see the potential in raising cattle on the recently vacated grasslands.

Antoine de Vallombrosa, the Marquis de Mores, was a French nobleman who had learned of the open-range grazing potential of the western Dakota grasslands from informants and written accounts appearing in the eastern United States. With financial backing from his wealthy father-in-law, Louis A. von Hoffman, a Wall Street banker, de Mores was able to acquire thousands of acres of land to start his new enterprise along the Little Missouri River. Prior to de Mores arriving in the area, a small collection of buildings on the west bank of the Little Missouri River called Little Missouri by most and Little Misery by some, was the earliest attempt at settlement. Also located on the west bank was the Badlands Cantonment, a military post established to protect railroad workers from marauding Native Americans.

Within a year of his arrival, de Mores started another community east of Little Missouri on the opposite bank, and named it after his wife, Medora, who was known as the Marquise de Mores. By 1885, the new community took precedence over the Little Missouri settlement. De Mores also built a ranch house, or chateau, as it was called by the locals, overlooking the river valley southwest of Medora. The chateau, with original furnishings, survives and is managed as a state historic site.

De Mores would also build a large meat packing plant on the east bank of the river to process grass-fed cattle for shipment to large volume markets. Another short-lived enterprise was the establishment of a stagecoach line between Medora and Deadwood, South Dakota. For a variety of reasons, including a murder trial in which he was the central figure, de Mores's badlands enterprises failed and he left the region and America in 1887 to pursue other interests abroad. De Mores was killed by Tuareg tribesmen in North Africa in 1896. He was 38 years old at the time of his death.

At age 25, Theodore Roosevelt arrived at Little Missouri at 3:00 a.m. on September 8, 1883, with intentions of bagging one of the few remaining bison. While still in the east, Roosevelt was informed of the country and wildlife in western Dakota Territory by Henry Gorringe who had assumed control of the Badlands Cantonment structures in early 1883. Roosevelt was soon to meet his objective, but not until after a long and tiring hunt which succeeded only because of his persistence. While hunting in the badlands, Roosevelt met and discussed the open-range cattle industry with several of the small ranchers with whom he came in contact. Most important of these was Gregor Lang. Roosevelt was soon smitten by the rugged country and impressed by the potential the area offered the prospective stockman. Later that month in St. Paul, Minnesota, he entered into an agreement with two Medora area locals, Sylvane Ferris and William Merrifield, to place some 400 head of cattle on what was called the Chimney Butte Ranch south of Medora. This ranch was also known as the Maltese Cross Ranch after the cattle brand Roosevelt used there. The following year, he established another ranch called the Elkhorn some 35 miles north of Medora.

There were profits to be made in the open range cattle industry in the early 1880s. However, disaster in the form of one of the worst winters on record struck in 1886–1887. Roosevelt, de Mores, and others suffered devastating losses to their herds. Some writers describe Roosevelt's losses as up to 60 percent of his herds. After the bad winter, Roosevelt was to annually spend short periods of time in the badlands from 1887 through 1894, and again in 1896. By 1897, however, the numbers of his cattle had dwindled and he decided to sell out. His political star was rising and he was newly remarried at this time. It is likely that he would not have found much time to devote to his ranching enterprises had the terrible winter not occurred.

In 1900, he was elected vice president of the United States, and less than a year later, when an assassin's bullet ended the life of Pres. William McKinley, he became president at age 42, the youngest man in history to assume that office.

After becoming president, Roosevelt visited North Dakota five times in 1903, 1910, 1911, 1912, and 1918. During his visit in 1903, he was able to renew old acquaintances when he spoke at the Medora Town Hall in April.

Roosevelt died unexpectedly at his home at Sagamore Hill in New York on January 6, 1919, three months after his last trip to North Dakota. He was 60 years old.

The evolution of Medora is characterized by a number of phases including the rapid initial development period of 1883 to 1885, when the town was booming; the equally rapid decline after the closure of the de Mores packing plant in the late 1880s; a transitional phase from the 1890s to the early 1950s when the National Park Service moved its park headquarters to Medora and began installing facilities in the park; the completion of the Burning Hills Amphitheater in 1958; and the Harold Schafer-Gold Seal Company phase beginning in 1962 when tourism-related reconstruction began. The latter phase evolved into management by the Theodore Roosevelt Medora Foundation. The park and community improvement aspects continue and will undoubtedly enhance visitor experiences well into the future.

As early as 1921, efforts were being made to establish a national park in the badlands near Medora to commemorate Roosevelt's badlands ranching days. In 1946, a portion of the badlands was designated a national wildlife refuge. Efforts to designate a national park in the badlands continued until 1947, when the south and elkhorn units of Theodore Roosevelt National Memorial Park were legislatively established. The following year, the north unit of the park, which is located near Watford City, was added. The three park units total approximately 110 square miles.

Medora is located immediately adjacent to the south unit park entrance and is accessed via Interstate Highway 94. Park headquarters are located at Medora. The north unit is located 15 miles south of Watford City adjacent to U.S. Highway 85.

In 1978, nearly 30 years after its establishment, the park was designated Theodore Roosevelt National Park and some portions of both the north and south units were included as components of the National Wilderness Preservation System. The name change gave the park greater recognition in the hierarchy of the National Park System and also provided recognition for the diversity of natural and cultural features found within the park units.

One

SETTLEMENTS PREDATING MEDORA

I must say that here, in this country of hills and plateaus, the romance of my life began.

—Theodore Roosevelt

The settlement called Little Missouri, Dakota Territory, predated Medora and was located on the west side of the Little Missouri River. It was here that 25-year-old Theodore Roosevelt disembarked from a Northern Pacific Railroad train to begin a buffalo hunt in September 1883. The Northern Pacific depot is pictured in the foreground. In the background is the Pyramid Park Hotel, run by Frank Moore, where Roosevelt spent his first night in Dakota Territory. (Photograph by F. Jay Haynes; courtesy of the State Historical Society of North Dakota 0119-17.)

This view looking to the south depicts the Northern Pacific Railroad crossing of the Little Missouri River and the settlement on the west bank known as Little Missouri as it appeared in 1880. The cabin of E. G. "Gerry" Paddock, one of the first white settlers in the area, is in the foreground. The photographer, F. Jay Haynes, was the official photographer for both Yellowstone National Park and the Northern Pacific Railroad. He had a special railroad car to transport his photographic equipment. The car would often be parked on a railroad siding where he was either awaiting customers or photographing nearby attractions along the route of the railroad. (Photograph by F. Jay Haynes; courtesy of Doug Ellison, Western Edge Books.)

Photographer F. Jay Haynes captured an image of soldiers standing at attention outside the Badlands Cantonment during exercises in 1880. The cantonment was located on the west side of the Little Missouri River near the Little Missouri settlement. The purpose of this military establishment was to protect workers on the Northern Pacific Railroad from Native American attacks. Railroad workers had reached the Little Missouri River and constructed a bridge by late September 1880. The cantonment was abandoned by the military in 1883. (Photograph by F. Jay Haynes; courtesy of the National Park Service.)

The Badlands Cantonment was located in the bottom lands of the Little Missouri River approximately three quarters of a mile northwest of what later became the community of Medora. This photograph is believed to have been taken either in 1879 or 1880. The cantonment was established in 1879 and disbanded in 1883, about the time Theodore Roosevelt and the Marquis de Mores arrived in the area. A plan was devised a short time after the military had abandoned the cantonment structures to convert them into a tourist resort from which to launch hunting parties. The venture was short lived. (Photograph by Morrow; courtesy of the State Historical Society of North Dakota 0087-02.)

Two

MEDORA THROUGH THE YEARS

It was a land of vast, silent spaces, of lonely rivers, and of plains, where the wild game stared at the passing horseman.

—Theodore Roosevelt

Medora was established in 1883 by a French nobleman, the Marquis de Mores. De Mores named the community after his attractive wife, Medora. By 1886, when this photograph was taken, a small collection of buildings and the de Mores packing plant, seen on the left middle ground, had already been constructed. This is one of the earliest extant views of Medora. The photograph appears to have been taken from near the base of cemetery hill, looking east. (Photograph by L. A. Huffman; courtesy of the Montana State Historical Society.)

There were only a few widely spaced buildings in Medora during the 1880s. St. Mary's Catholic Church, constructed from funding provided by the Marquise de Mores, is recognizable in the left background. (Photograph by F. Jay Haynes; courtesy of the Montana State Historical Society.)

Even as late as 1902, when this photograph was taken, very few buildings existed at the Medora town site. A number of buildings had left Medora for Dickinson on Northern Pacific Railroad flat cars after the demise of the de Mores packing plant. This view was taken looking to the northwest, with the Northern Pacific Railroad tracks and depot in the middle ground, the de Mores packing plant and brick stack are visible in the left background, and St. Mary's Catholic Church is in the right background. (Photograph by Elliott W. Hunter; courtesy of the Montana State Historical Society.)

This image is perhaps one of the first photographs taken of the Metropolitan Hotel, later named the Rough Riders Hotel. Note the new lumber and unpainted walls. The photograph is from an old cabinet card collected by Lulu Cornell, from rural Medora. (Courtesy of the Leppart collection.)

The Northern Pacific Railroad depot at Medora burned on April 10, 1925. The fire was created by sparks from a passing train combined with high winds. The effect of the wind seems apparent in this photograph. (Courtesy of the National Park Service.)

A significant segment of the population of Medora is shown standing outside the original De Mores Hotel in this wintry looking scene. The hotel was built in 1883 and managed by George W. Fitzgerald. Fitzgerald managed the establishment until January 1885, when he started construction of his own hotel which was first named the Metropolitan and later renamed the Rough Riders in 1903. The Marquis de Mores later extensively remodeled this building, even to the extent of placing it on a new foundation, and had it faced with brick veneer. (Courtesy of the State Historical Society of North Dakota 0615-04.)

The De Mores Hotel (also known as the Northern Pacific Hotel) burned September 12, 1897. A few items of furniture were taken from the building before flames consumed the hotel and contents. The photographer and date of this photograph are unknown, but it is quite likely that the photograph was taken in the 1880s given the new appearance of the building. (Courtesy of the National Park Service.)

The banner was hung on the De Mores Hotel on January 6, 1896, as a result of a trial that occurred in Bismarck the previous month. Two individuals from Billings County were acquitted of a murder, which occurred some 20 miles north of Medora. "May You Roast In Hell Hutch" refers to the jury foreman whose last name was Hutchinson. Some Medora-area residents were obviously not happy with the verdict. (Courtesy of the Leppart collection.)

These two views of the Northern Pacific Railroad depot at Medora were probably taken around the same time. Note the crate of elk antlers about to be shipped off to some distant point (right foreground) and the section hand cart to the left in the top photograph. (Above, courtesy of the Leppart photograph collection; below, courtesy of the Montana State Historical Society.)

Some of the most common views found in Medora historical photography are those photographs taken from the bluffs overlooking the community from the north and east. The von Hoffman house is clearly visible in the lower left corner. This early view dated July 31, 1924, was taken by Paul Lebo, a Medora resident. (Lebo photograph; courtesy of the Leppart collection.)

This is an early photograph of Medora taken from cemetery hill some time before paved roads reached the community. The Red Trail (left) and Northern Pacific Railroad bridges are visible in the middle ground. The Red Trail was a predecessor of U.S. Highway 10. The name originated from the use of clinker rock as road surfacing material. The rock originates from underground burning coal veins baking the overlying clays into natural brick, red to pink in coloration, which is regionally called scoria. (Courtesy of the Leppart collection.)

Another photographic vantage point used by individuals is from cemetery hill which is located southwest of the community. Similar photographs have been described as aerial views of Medora, but the photographers did indeed have their feet on the ground. U.S. Highway 10 and the Northern Pacific Railroad bridges crossing the Little Missouri River are in the right foreground. The date of this photograph is unknown, but it was possibly taken in the 1940s or 1950s. (Courtesy of the Leppart collection.)

This photograph provides an expansive view of Medora from the east bluff. Note the horses grazing in the middle foreground and the rustic log cabin Texaco station in the upper left. The open expanse in the middle foreground is now occupied by the Badlands Motel, the Medora Community Center, the Billings County Courthouse, the Billings County Historical Museum, Western Edge Book Store, and other structures. (Courtesy of the Leppart collection.)

This is a closer view of the log cabin Texaco station. This photograph is dated October 1961. The structure was dismantled a few years later when a portion of the Badlands Motel was constructed on the site. (Courtesy of the Leppart collection.)

These three connected buildings were the Northern Pacific Refrigerated Car Company's general store (center building) and offices built by the Marquis de Mores in 1883. The building on the left continues to exist in Medora, close to its original location. It has been placed on a foundation, re-sided, and a deck and entryway were added as part of living quarters that have been used for many years. It is believed by the author to be the oldest building in Medora. (Courtesy of the State Historical Society of North Dakota 098-24.)

ROUGH RIDER HOTEL, MEDORA, N

The most recognizable building in Medora in early photographs as well as present day, is the Rough Riders Hotel. The centerpiece of Medora has always been the hotel. This early view shows a small crowd of people in front of the structure. A number of individuals are on horseback

...hich is befitting this "old west" community. (Photograph by Doubleday–Myers; courtesy of ...Vally Owen, Indergaard family collection.)

The old hotel fell into disrepair over the years. This view was taken March 29, 1948, by George Grant. The Rough Riders Hotel was constructed by George Fitzgerald in 1884 and 1885. Hotel dimensions were 35-feet-by-80-feet. The *Badlands Cowboy* newspaper reported on December 4, 1884, that the hotel was to be finished by January 15, 1885. The hotel was first called the Metropolitan but later renamed the Rough Riders Hotel in 1903 to commemorate the Theodore Roosevelt Rough Riders of the Spanish-American War. (Courtesy of the National Park Service.)

Tourist rooms were available in Medora on a limited scale when this photograph was taken, possibly in the 1940s. The sign is symbolic of the major tourist attraction Medora has become. (Courtesy of Wally Owen, Indergaard family collection.)

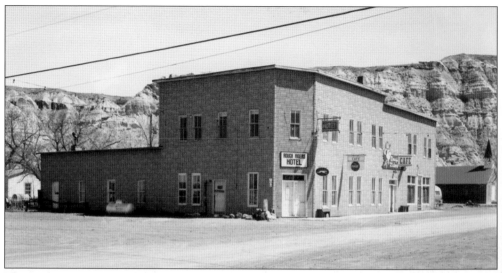

This is the appearance of the Rough Riders Hotel shortly before reconstruction was started by the Gold Seal Company of Bismarck. The photograph was taken April 1961. (Photograph by Dick Maeder; courtesy of the National Park Service.)

Roy Mallory and David Leppart stand near the entrance to the Rough Riders Hotel in th[e] June 1956, image. The hotel was also the Greyhound bus stop for many years. (Courtesy of th[e] Leppart collection.)

The Rough Riders Hotel was reconstructed during the early 1960s. It was during the 1960s that a great deal of reconstruction, conducted by the Gold Seal Company of Bismarck, occurred in Medora. (Courtesy of the National Park Service.)

The Rough Riders Hotel reconstruction was completed and the facility was opened to the public in 1964. It was then owned and operated by the Gold Seal Company of Bismarck. (Photograph by North Dakota Tourism Department; courtesy of the Leppart collection.)

Jim Barnhart was proprietor of the Log Cabin Saloon when this photograph was taken. The Log Cabin Saloon and the Cave Bar were favorite social centers in the community. (Courtesy of the National Park Service.)

he Log Cabin Saloon location is now known as the Badlands Pizza Parlor and Saloon. This notograph dates from March 11, 1964. The building is located west of the Rough Riders Hotel. Photograph by Einar Johnson; courtesy of the National Park Service.)

The Joe Ferris Store was built in early 1885. Joe Ferris was one of the first individuals Theodore Roosevelt met at Little Missouri. Ferris was one of the first individuals contacted by Theodore Roosevelt after arriving at Little Missouri and served as his guide during the 1883 bison hunt. He also served as Roosevelt's guide on a bison hunt in 1883. The structure dimensions were 25-feet-by-75-feet. On August 13, 1885, the *Badlands Cowboy* newspaper carried the first advertisement for the Ferris Store. This photograph was taken in April 1961. The Ferris Store has since been reconstructed by the Gold Seal Company. (Photograph by Dick Maeder; courtesy of the National Park Service.)

U.S. Highway 10 once took travelers through the heart of Medora years before the construction of Interstate Highway 94. This view is believed to have been taken in the 1940s, and clearly shows the Rough Riders Hotel, which is the white building in the background. (Courtesy of the National Park Service.)

Three unidentified early Medora residents are seen doing a little clowning around in this view with a blacksmith shop and clubroom providing the backdrop. The LZ clubhouse was a local entertainment establishment during the early part of the 20th century that provided alcohol and was the frequent scene of numerous poker games. Johnnie Britt was the proprietor.

Conrad "Dutch" Ziegler (left) and Chris Rasmussen pose for the camera near the Medora Northern Pacific depot. Both of these individuals spent many years in the Medora area. Rasmussen's former ranch lands are now included in the south unit of Theodore Roosevelt National Park. (Courtesy of the Leppart collection.)

Medora area residents never forgot that the 26th president of the United States, Theodore Roosevelt, once ranched in the valley of the Little Missouri River. The Little Missouri River was designated a state scenic river by the North Dakota legislature in the late 1970s. It is the only river in the state of North Dakota to be so designated. The Red Trail Bridge is visible in the background. (Courtesy of the Leppart collection.)

A statue of the Marquis de Mores was placed in a central location in the De Mores Memorial Park in June 1926. Dedication of the statue was held a year later as the statue was damaged by vandals setting fire to a canvas covering shortly after it was placed in the park. The Vallombrosa brothers, Louis and Paul, sons of the Marquis and Marquise de Mores, commissioned the full-length bronze statue of their father. The statue and granite stone base were shipped from Paris, France, to Medora. The Rough Riders Hotel is visible in the background. (Courtesy of the Leppart collection.)

Thick tree and shrubbery growth have obscured the view of buildings surrounding the De Mores Memorial Park over the years. Landscaping for the park was conducted by the Works Progress Administration (WPA) and included a stone wall and hand-hammered ornamental iron ckets. The park area was deeded to the Medora Civil Township by the Vallombrosa brothers 1925. The statue of the Marquis de Mores stands alone, near the center of the community the enchman founded in 1883. (Courtesy of the Leppart collection.)

Construction of the Billings County Courthouse was completed in 1913. This building has been replaced with a new courthouse that would be the envy of many communities, including those much larger than Medora. The building is currently used as the Billings County Historical Museum and is on the National Register of Historic Places. (Courtesy of the State Historical Society of North Dakota 0259-07.)

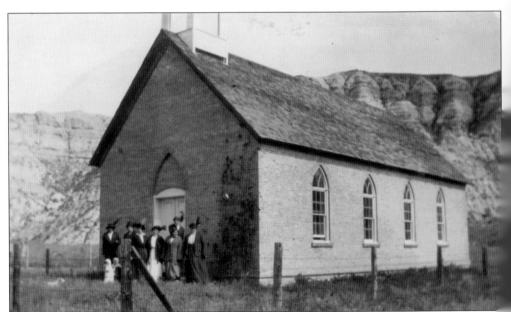

St. Mary's Catholic Church was constructed from funding provided by the Marquise de More. The cornerstone of the church was laid on September 20, 1884, and the first mass celebrated o November 2, 1884. The church can still be seen in its original location. It holds the distinctio of being the oldest Catholic church still in use in North Dakota. The building was included o the National Register of Historic Places in 1977. (Courtesy of the Leppart collection.)

This is a view of the west-central portion of Medora looking to the north. This photograph is believed to have been taken in the 1950s prior to the construction of the south unit park access road that cut through the bluff on the left side of this image. The Corner Cafe is immediately behind the power pole, Brown's Gift Shop is behind the café, and the Ferris Store (left background) and Rough Riders Hotel (right background) are visible. (Courtesy of the State Historical Society of North Dakota 0743-23.)

The town site of Medora was developed on a portion of the Little Missouri River floodplain. The plant community, which favored the sandy alluvial soils along the river, was partly comprised of cottonwood trees. Two of the native cottonwood trees were allowed to grow old in Medora streets. This tree became a hazard and was removed in 1995. It was located northeast of the De Mores School. Another very old cottonwood tree grows in the street in front of the Medora bank and post office. That tree appears in all of the early photographs the author has examined which include that section of Medora. See the photograph at the top of page 19. (Courtesy of the State Historical Society of North Dakota 0042-029.)

A young cowboy rides his horse near the present-day location of the Western Edge Bookstore in this vintage photograph. The tree in the background is the one removed in 1995, northeast of the De Mores School. (Courtesy of the National Park Service.)

The three-story brick De Mores School building served the educational needs of Medora and the surrounding ranching community for many years. It was demolished in 1986 when a new school building was completed. (Photograph by George Grant; courtesy of the National Park Service.)

The von Hoffman house was constructed in 1884 by the Marquis de Mores as a guesthouse for his in-laws. It was also later the home of James W. Foley, who published some 13 volumes of poetry and became North Dakota's poet laureate. In more recent years, it became a museum, and eventually a doll house that displays late-19th and early-20th-century dolls and other antique toys. This building can still be seen in Medora. It was placed on the National Register of Historic Places in 1977. (Courtesy of the Leppart collection.)

Many photographers used the east bluff for photographing the community. This is another such photograph. The von Hoffman house is visible in the lower-right foreground. It is the house with the two tall chimneys. The photographer and date are unknown, but the image probably dates from the early 1900s. (Courtesy of the State Historical Society of North Dakota 0259-03.)

This is one of the better panoramic views of Medora, taken in 1886. Notable buildings visible are the von Hoffman house in the lower-left corner, St. Mary's Catholic Church in the middle foreground, and a little further to the right and above the church is the unpainted Metropolitan Hotel (later Rough Riders Hotel). The persistent cottonwood tree is immediately below, to the east of the hotel. Also identifiable in this photograph are the three adjacent Northern Pacific Refrigerator Car Company's general store and offices in the left middle ground. In the right background is the de Mores packing plant and to the upper left, the de Mores chateau can be seen. (Courtesy of the State Historical Society of North Dakota B0484.)

This image appears on an old cabinet photograph card and was originally collected by Lulu Cornell of rural Medora. This good quality image is of the interior of the Joe Ferris store and was obviously taken by a professional photographer of the day. The photographer and date of the photograph are unknown. The period clothing is representative of the early 1900s. (Courtesy of the Leppart collection.)

The Joe Ferris store has been replaced by a reconstructed building. According to the walking tour guidebook titled *Footsteps Into Medora's Past,* Theodore Roosevelt stayed overnight in a room above the original store from time to time. (Courtesy of the State Historical Society of North Dakota 0739-VI-p33e.)

A photograph of Medora in the winter, copyright 1926, was undoubtedly taken much earlier since the de Mores packing plant, visible in the lower left, is present. The photograph probably dates from the late 1800s or early 1900s. The packing plant burned on March 17, 1907. (Courtesy of the Leppart collection.)

Livestock, including both horses and cattle, were allowed to roam on the unoccupied portions of the town site for many years. Feral goats occupied the bluffs overlooking Medora well into the 1950s. (Courtesy of the Leppart collection.)

The boy in the foreground is Albert Leo Brown, an early resident of Medora, and in later years, a resident of Livingston, Montana. This photograph probably dates from the 1940s. The white building in the background is the Rough Riders Hotel. (Courtesy of the Leppart collection.)

The late Ralph "Doc" Hubbard (left) posed with world champion trick roper the late Jim Eskew from Oklahoma, in this photograph. Eskew performed in Medora for several summer seasons. Ralph Hubbard was the son of the late Elbert Hubbard of Roycrofter fame, who perished during the sinking of the Lusitania. Ralph was a well-known authority on Native American crafts and a celebrity in his own right. (Photograph by Ernest Feland; courtesy of the Leppart collection.)

The dedication of the Red Trail Bridge across the Little Missouri River in 1914 brought many local citizens to the bridge site, as seen below. The bridge was later removed and cut up for scrap. A modern concrete bridge has replaced the old metal one. (Above, courtesy of Wally Owen, Indergaard family collection; below, courtesy of the State Historical Society of North Dakota 0259-12.)

First School House in Medora where Jimmie Foley taught. © 1926

The photograph caption tells it all except that Jimmie Foley was James W. Foley, North Dakota's poet laureate, who also taught school in Medora. There were very few students available to attend school at Medora, and combined grades were not uncommon for many years. (Courtesy of the Leppart collection.)

The Ray house was one of the more stately early Medora residences. The building can still be seen on the eastern edge of Medora and is easily recognizable since few changes in outward appearance have occurred. (Courtesy of the Leppart collection.)

The Lebo house was built close to the bluff on the east side of Medora. Norman Lebo was a cook and teamster for Theodore Roosevelt during a hunting trip to the Bighorn Mountains in August and September 1884. Roosevelt remarked of Lebo that he "possessed a most extraordinary stock of miscellaneous mis-information upon every conceivable subject." (Courtesy of the Leppart collection.)

Earl Bird rides his paint horse past the old Medora Post Office in this undated photograph. This building was later removed and a new post office was constructed approximately one block away. (Photograph by Chester Brooks; courtesy of the National Park Service.)

The community is well-known for impressive Fourth of July parades, despite the fact that the population has hovered around 100 for decades. This is an entry in the 1946 parade. (Photograph by Leo D. Harris; courtesy of the Leppart collection.)

Jim Barnhart carries a large U.S. flag and leads the parade down Highway 10, a short distance west of Medora in this 1946 view. This photograph was taken immediately east of the highway bridge crossing the Little Missouri River. (Courtesy of the Leppart collection.)

Identifiable individuals in the 1946 parade are Jim Barnhart with the U.S. flag and Paul Lebo in the cart next to the stagecoach. Lebo was handicapped, but despite this he became an excellent photographer. A number of his images are included in this book. (Courtesy of the Leppart collection.)

The large dark building (center) is the billiard hall built by Bob Roberts, proprietor of Big Mouthed Bob's Bug Juice Dispensary at Little Missouri. The building was also called the "old red hall" and was dismantled in 1923. St. Mary's Catholic Church, built from funding provided by the Marquise de Mores, can be seen in the right background, directly behind the pole. The Metropolitan Hotel (later Rough Riders Hotel) can also be seen in the left background. (Courtesy of the State Historical Society of North Dakota 0615-02.)

Big Mouthed Bob's Bug Juice Dispensary was moved from Little Missouri to the first floor of this building. The first floor was also used as a roller skating rink during the winter months. The building was located in the general vicinity of the old Medora Town Hall. It also became the first Billings County Courthouse. (Courtesy of the National Park Service.)

Three

THE BURNING HILLS AMPHITHEATER

Only those are fit to live who do not fear to die; and none are fit to die who have shrunk from the joy of life. Both life and death are parts of the same great adventure.

—Theodore Roosevelt

The Burning Hills Amphitheater was built into the side of a bluff approximately one mile southwest of Medora in the late 1950s, largely through volunteer labor. The initial presentation at the outdoor venue was titled *Old Four Eyes*. The title represented what some individuals nicknamed Theodore Roosevelt because of his need to wear spectacles. The outdoor shows began in 1958, with a seating capacity for 1,500 individuals. (Courtesy of the National Park Service.)

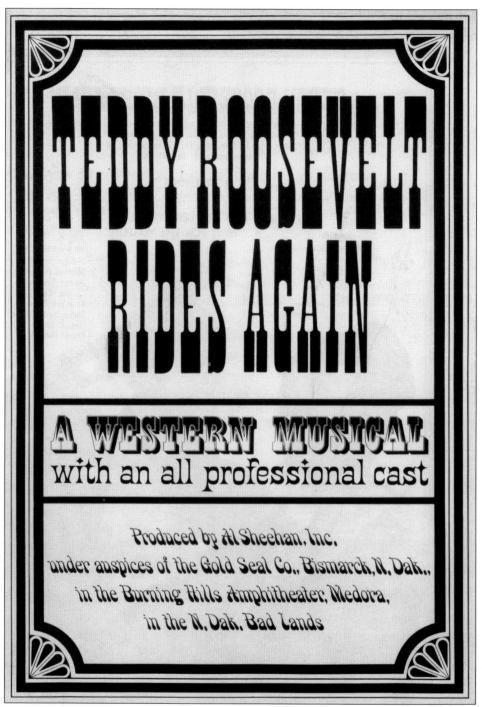

TEDDY ROOSEVELT RIDES AGAIN

A WESTERN MUSICAL
with an all professional cast

Produced by Al Sheehan, Inc.,
under auspices of the Gold Seal Co., Bismarck, N. Dak.,
in the Burning Hills Amphitheater, Medora,
in the N. Dak. Bad Lands

A variety of presentations occurred at the amphitheater over the years under the auspices of the Gold Seal Company of Bismarck. There were musical programs as well as variety acts. Most presentations had a central patriotic theme commemorating Theodore Roosevelt's ranching days in the badlands. The programs proved very popular with the public. The venue is now known as the Medora Musical. (Courtesy of Wally Owen, Indergaard family collection.)

A moment in time was captured when the photographer clicked his shutter on a barroom scene during the early years of the *Old Four Eyes* show. A number of local individuals appeared in the *Old Four Eyes* presentation. (Courtesy of the National Park Service.)

The early 1960s saw Dave Lommen (left) and Bill Bail, who were actors in the *Old Four Eyes* show. Actors were recruited from all over the United States. (Photograph by W. P. Sebens, North Dakota Soil Conservation Committee; courtesy of the Leppart collection.)

A mock branding scene from the *Old Four Eyes* show is depicted in this view. Theodore Roosevelt did participate in real branding activity while in the Dakota badlands. (Photograph by W. P. Sebens, North Dakota Soil Conservation Committee; courtesy of the Leppart collection.)

Theodore Roosevelt, played by Dave Lommen (left), meets Joe Murdock, played by Bill Bail, at the Northern Pacific depot in Medora. The Burning Hills Amphitheater is now equipped with comfortable seating and an escalator. (Photograph by W. P. Sebens, North Dakota Soil Conservation Committee; courtesy of the Leppart collection.)

Four

MEDORA RODEOS

I have been three weeks on the roundup and have worked as hard as any
of the cowboys. Yesterday, I was eighteen hours in the saddle.

—Theodore Roosevelt

Rodeo events were a natural for the old west town of Medora, and annual rodeos were held near the community for many years. The earliest rodeo grounds were located south of the railroad tracks, which are clearly visible in this view, near where the Medora stockyards are currently located. The bluffs, which overlook Medora on the north, are visible in the background. Rodeo spectators were able to stand just outside their automobiles to watch the action since they were allowed to drive to the edge of the elliptically-shaped rodeo grounds. (Courtesy of Wally Owen, Undergaard family collection.)

During the earliest days of rodeo at Medora, the grounds were left natural, sporting sagebrush, grass, and perhaps a little prickly pear cactus. These steer-wrestling images were by Doubleday-Myers, famous photographers of many rodeo events throughout the western United States. The firm sold many such images in the form of real-photo postcards. (Courtesy of the Leppart collection.)

Hundreds of rodeo images were taken during the first quarter of the 20th century. Many are of poor quality or the subjects were too far away when the camera shutter was released. This image is an exception. The action of the horse has been stopped, the subject is close, and the image is relatively sharp given the technology of the time. (Photograph by Doubleday; courtesy of the Leppart collection.)

Rodeo events were a spin-off of some everyday ranching tasks, such as roping and riding, that were presented in a far more dramatic manner than normally occurred on the ranch. Rodeos were obviously popular with area residents during the early part of the 20th century as evidenced by the large number of automobiles and people visible in this view. It was also an opportune time for individuals who lived in a sparsely settled part of the country to get together and visit. (Photograph by W. R. Collis; courtesy of the Leppart collection.)

"HOOK 'EM COW"
FRONTIER DAYS, MEDORA, N.D.
DOUBLEDAY-MYERS
PHOTO

Riding skills that were developed on the ranch were sometimes employed for humorous entertainment rather than competition during some of the early rodeos. In later years, the rodeo grounds were moved to a small valley northwest of the de Mores chateau, immediately south of what became the Burning Hills Amphitheater. Competition for cash awards has always been what rodeo is all about. (Photograph by Doubleday-Myers; courtesy of the Leppart collection.)

BARE BACK RIDING, MEDORA, N, D, "DOUBLEDAY-MYERS" PHOTO

Bareback bronc riding, saddle bronc riding, and steer wrestling or bulldogging as it was sometimes called were obviously favorite events of rodeo fans. Conspicuously absent are the rodeo clowns that would be present at today's rodeos wherever bull riding is a contestant sport. (Photograph by Doubleday-Myers; courtesy of the Leppart collection.)

FRONTIER DAYS, MEDORA, N.D.
"DOUBLEDAY MYERS"

Southwestern North Dakota is well-known for producing world-champion caliber rodeo contestants such as Alvin Nelson and brothers Jim and Tom Tescher during the last half of the 20th century. The North Dakota Cowboy Hall of Fame was established at Medora to recognize North Dakota's rodeo cowboys and others who have notably contributed to the western way of life. (Photographs by Doubleday-Myers; courtesy of the Leppart collection.)

"GARDNER" RIDING A BUCKING DEVIL."
DOUBLEDAY MYERS PHOTO

Some rodeo photographers became quite famous after many years of taking pictures. This is certainly true of the Doubleday-Myers team. These photographers were recognized by a feature article in *Persimmon Hill*, a publication of the National Cowboy and Western Heritage Museum in Oklahoma City. (Photographs by Doubleday-Myers; courtesy of the Leppart collection.)

Five

PAINTED CANYON AND CEDAR CANYON SCENIC OVERLOOKS

I know so many of you here and it seems good to breathe this free Western air again.

—Theodore Roosevelt

In 1964, this was a familiar scene at the Painted Canyon tourist stop east of Medora. The structures were built on the edge of a bluff overlooking the badlands, approximately six miles east of Medora. The visitor facilities consisted of a restaurant (first building beyond the chapel), cages for captive animals, a gift shop, and a residence occupied by Roy and June Noyes. The roadway had scoria surfacing and the road edge was lined with petrified wood stumps collected from nearby areas of the badlands. Roy advertised his restaurant as having the best homemade pies between Miles City and Dickinson. None of these structures exist at this location today. (Courtesy of the National Park Service.)

Many travelers who visited the badlands in the 1950s and 1960s would recognize this view of the restaurant and dining area at Painted Canyon. A few animal cages are also visible at the right edge of this photograph. Native wildlife was displayed here and included an enclosure with a number of rattlesnakes that frequently attracted visitor attention. (Courtesy of Wally Owen, Indergaard family collection.)

Betty Cornell greets visitors from Dickinson from a window serving outside guests. Cornell provided home-baked pastries and meals at the Painted Canyon facility for many years. (Courtesy of the Leppart collection.)

A turnout from U.S. Highway 10 was located immediately east of the Painted Canyon Restaurant and other structures, seen above. Visitors were able to drive to the edge of the bluff for spectacular views of the badlands. The turnout was bordered by a rock wall and a small observation shelter constructed of badlands clinker rock, seen below. The clinkers formed in underground burning coal veins. (Above, photograph by Osborn, Dickinson; both photographs courtesy of the Leppart collection.)

Two very early views of the structures at the Painted Canyon overlook are featured on real-photo postcards. The photograph at the top of this page is presumably the older image based on the sparse signage and what might be the rudimentary beginnings of the building shown in the lower photograph. Both images reveal the liberal use of local clinker rock in building construction. The Painted Canyon Overlook depicted in these photographs was replaced by modern restroom facilities and a small visitor information center constructed by the National Park Service in the late 1970s as part of the development of Interstate Highway 94. The interstate highway replaced U.S. Highway 10. (Below, photograph by Osborn, Dickinson; both photographs courtesy of the Leppart collection.)

The Cedar Canyon facilities consisted of a small gift shop in the southern part of the building with a residence in the back or north side. The structure was faced with clinker rock, much like the buildings at Painted Canyon. Cedar Canyon was also located along U.S. Highway 10, approximately one mile east of Painted Canyon. A guided motorized tour of a petrified forest in Cedar Canyon was available for a number of years. The Cedar Canyon facilities were removed during construction of Interstate Highway 94, and the area was rehabilitated to appear as natural as possible. (Photograph by Osborn, Dickinson; courtesy of the Leppart collection.)

Visitors pose in front of the Park Trading Post at Cedar Canyon. Marvin and Helen Ingman were the last proprietors of the trading post. Their business was later moved to Medora. (Courtesy of the Leppart collection.)

Two views of the rugged Cedar Canyon area are featured in these early real-photo postcards. The distant horizons in both views are visible from nearby Painted Canyon. (Above photograph by Paul Lebo; both images courtesy of Leppart collection.)

Six

THEODORE ROOSEVELT IN THE BADLANDS

The Nation behaves well if it treats the natural resources as assets which it must turn over to the next generation increased, and not impaired, in value.

—Theodore Roosevelt

There are several images similar to this one of Theodore Roosevelt taken while he was ranching in the North Dakota Badlands during the early 1880s. Two of the images are of Roosevelt standing next to his horse as in this photograph, and others show him seated on the horse. Roosevelt was considered to be a dude by some of the locals and sometimes dressed the part. It was not long, however, before he was able to prove himself equal to the task of rancher and novice cowboy. (Courtesy of the Leppart collection.)

Theodore Roosevelt spent about 359 days in the North Dakota Badlands between 1883 and 1887. In this view, he is dressed in buckskins and is posing for a studio portrait taken in New York after returning from his first trip west. Roosevelt memorabilia is on display for today's visitors at the park service visitor center in Medora. (Courtesy of the Leppart collection.)

Roosevelt's presidential train passed through western North Dakota in 1903. On April 7, Roosevelt addressed a gathering of friends and former neighbors at the Medora Town Hall when this photograph was taken. It was during this stop that he was able to renew old acquaintances with area residents. (Courtesy of the National Park Service.)

Theodore Roosevelt's horse, Manitou, was photographed at Dickinson. The smudges on this real-photo postcard are the result of a Little Missouri River flood that damaged a number of photographs stored by Lulu Cornell in the Cornell ranch house. The Little Missouri remains a free-flowing river. (Courtesy of the Leppart collection.)

Roosevelt's log cabin from the Maltese Cross Ranch was originally located approximately seven miles south of Medora on the east side of the Little Missouri River. The cabin was later purchased by the State of North Dakota in 1903 and exhibited at the 1904 St. Louis World's Fair. The cabin was then sent to the 1905 Lewis and Clark Exposition in Portland, Oregon. After the Lewis and Clark centennial event, it was sent to Fargo where it was used as an exhibit at the State Fair Grounds in 1906 and 1907. From 1908 to 1959, it stood on the capitol grounds in Bismarck before being moved to Medora. For each move, with the exception of the move from Bismarck to Medora, it was disassembled and then reassembled log by log. (Courtesy of the Leppart collection.)

The Maltese Cross Ranch was Roosevelt's first ranch headquarters in the Little Missouri Badlands. It was also known as the Chimney Butte Ranch, named for a prominent butte located near the ranch headquarters a short distance west of the Little Missouri River. Both of Roosevelt's ranch cabins were a Spartan contrast to the home the Marquis de Mores built overlooking Medora. Theodore Roosevelt was well known for his preference for "roughing it." (Courtesy of the Leppart collection.)

The Maltese Cross cabin was moved to Medora in 1959 to a location immediately north of the park visitor center. The pine logs were then disassembled and treated with a preservative. The roof was also replaced to resemble the original high-pitched roof that was present when the cabin was on the ranch. A loft was added to replicate what was present when Roosevelt occupied the cabin. The outside dimensions of the cabin are 18-by-24-feet, which is much smaller than the Elkhorn Ranch house. The cabin was built for Roosevelt by Sylvane Ferris and William Merrifield. (Photograph by Bernard Weinreich; courtesy of the National Park Service.)

The cabin was moved intact from the capitol grounds at Bismarck to Medora. The cabin was disassembled and restoration measures were taken when it was placed at its current location near the park service visitor center in Medora. (Courtesy of the Leppart collection.)

The interior of Roosevelt's cabin is furnished with late-1800s items representative of Roosevelt's time in the badlands. A few of the items were used by Theodore Roosevelt. The cabin would have been heated by burning wood and lignite coal. Both fuel sources were available in or near the Little Missouri River bottoms. (Photographs by David H. Huntzinger; courtesy of the National Park Service.)

BY-LAWS

OF THE

LITTLE MISSOURI RIVER

Stockmen's Association

THEODORE ROOSEVELT, Chairman

HENRY S. BOICE, Vice-Chairman

PRESS OF

G. P. PUTNAM'S SONS

27 & 29 WEST 23D STREET, NEW YORK

1885

During his ranching days in the badlands, Roosevelt helped organize and was elected the first chairman of the Little Missouri River Stockmen's Association. Area ranchers also had enough confidence in Roosevelt to represent them at the Montana Stockmen's Association meetings held in Miles City, Montana. (Courtesy of the National Park Service.)

The setting for the Elkhorn Ranch headquarters on the west bank of the Little Missouri River was one of serenity. The old ranch site is located approximately 35 miles north of Medora. No structures remain at the site. (Photograph by Theodore Roosevelt; courtesy of the National Park Service.)

Theodore Roosevelt photographed the barns and corrals on the Elkhorn Ranch in the mid-1880s. Roosevelt was a careful observer and documented what he was seeing in his published accounts and by a limited use of photography. Roosevelt wrote more than 30 books, 10 of which were on the west. Parts of at least two books were written while he was at the Elkhorn Ranch. (Photograph by Theodore Roosevelt; courtesy of the National Park Service.)

Roosevelt recruited two former hunting companions from Maine to construct his second ranch headquarters. William "Bill" Sewall, pictured here many years later in Maine, was one of the builders of the Elkhorn Ranch headquarters. The other individual was Wilmot Dow. Both individuals were hardy Maine woodsmen. The ranch cabin at Elkhorn was larger than the Maltese Cross cabin, measuring 30-by-60 feet. Modern photographers would have moved their position so that the tree would not appear to be growing from the subject Sewall's head. (Courtesy of the National Park Service.)

BUFFALO HUNTERS CAMP, BILLINGS CO. N. DAK. COPYRIGHTED 1908 BY R. E. MCKIF

An old buffalo hunter's cabin that was once located not far from the Elkhorn Ranch is symbolic of the 1880s when Roosevelt came to the badlands to hunt bison. According to some naturalists, bison herds on the North American continent numbered some 30 million head at the onset of European expansion. By 1883, only remnants were left. One of the last herds in the region was found near Jordan, Montana, where a number of animals were collected by William T. Hornaday, chief taxidermist for the National Museum. (Photograph by R. E. McKibbin; courtesy of the Leppart collection.)

Seven

THE MARQUIS DE MORES

Every printed word, bore my brand. There were no mavericks in the Bad Lands Cowboy articles. There was no libel law; no law of any kind except six-shooter rights. And I was the only man who never carried a six-shooter.

—Arthur T. Packard, publisher of the *Badlands Cowboy*, Medora

Antoine de Vallombrosa, the Marquis de Mores, was a bold, colorful, and a somewhat flamboyant individual who stood out in the badlands community and elsewhere. He was controversial and not universally liked by all. He was very ambitious and with substantial financial backing, started a number of enterprises in a very short time while in the badlands. It was he who established the community of Medora and named the village after his wife. He became a large stakeholder in the early livestock grazing enterprises that were springing up in western Dakota Territory. He started a meat packing plant at Medora and also speculated in the marketing of salmon. (Courtesy of the National Park Service.)

From a Portrait of Marquise De Mores, Medora, N.D.

The original portrait of the Marquise de Mores portrayed on this postcard is housed at the State Heritage Center in Bismarck. A very good print copy can be seen at the chateau in Medora. The painting was sent from France in 1953 by one of the de Mores' sons. The community of Medora was named for the Marquise. (Courtesy of the Leppart collection.)

The Marquis de Mores and his wife were avid hunters. Many game species were still plentiful in Dakota Territory during the years the couple spent in the badlands. However, most of the large bison herds had been eliminated by 1883. (Photograph by E. R. Kennedy; courtesy of the National Park Service.)

The 26-room summer ranch home, or chateau as it was called by local individuals, was built by the Marquis de Mores in 1883 and continues to overlook the Medora community and the Little Missouri River valley. The structure and surrounding grounds are now a state historic site under the auspices of the State Historical Society of North Dakota. Original de Mores belongings that were used in the 1880s are on display at the chateau. The chateau is included in the National Register of Historic Places. (Courtesy of the Leppart collection.)

The de Mores party is ready to leave for a hunt in this view taken from the south side of the chateau. The Marquise de Mores is seated on a horse while riding sidesaddle (left center), while the Marquis stands to the right of the individuals pictured. (Courtesy of the National Park Service.)

The de Mores chateau has no doubt been photographed thousands of times since it was constructed in 1883. This unusual view includes the chimney from the de Mores packing plant in the background. (Courtesy of Doug Ellison, Western Edge Books.)

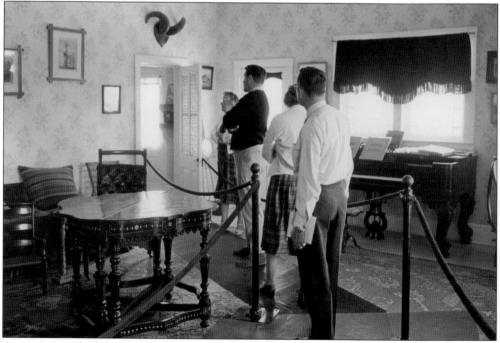

Anita Organ (far left) conducts a guided tour of the chateau in this 1960s vintage photograph. Some of the de Mores original furnishings are visible in this view. (Photograph by North Dakota Tourism Department; Leppart collection.)

This small stone structure was constructed of locally obtained petrified log sections with bison skulls imbedded in concrete on either side of the door. This building was located a short distance from the chateau veranda. Although the original purpose of the structure is not known, it was reportedly used as a playhouse at times by the chateau caretaker's children. (Photograph by Paul Lebo; courtesy of the Leppart collection.)

The veranda at the chateau was decorated with relics from the badlands and period furniture in this early view. Many old photographs of badlands ranch buildings include bison skulls hanging from walls or laying in yards. These skulls, remnants of the vast herds, were a common sight in the late 19th and early 20th centuries. For several years in the mid-1880s, individuals were able to conduct a thriving business by collecting bison bones and bringing them to collection points along the Northern Pacific Railroad for shipment to eastern processors. (Courtesy of Wally Owen, Indergaard family collection.)

The caption on this photograph states "de Mores at dinner on his Roundup," yet the Marquis de Mores is not readily identifiable in this image. Annual cattle roundups were conducted over the sprawling, unfenced rangelands in order to brand unmarked calves and corral cattle ready for market. De Mores hired a cowboy named John Goodall, who had been working in the Bighorn Basin of Wyoming, to serve as foreman for his ranching activities. This proved to be an excellent choice as Goodall became a notable Medora-area citizen and future sheriff of Stark County. (Courtesy of the Leppart collection.)

The Marquis de Mores has saddled his horse and is ready to travel in this view outside the chateau. The open window behind the Marquis probably indicates that this photograph was taken during a warm weather season. (Photograph provided by the North Dakota Tourism Department; courtesy of the Leppart collection.)

The de Mores packing plant was under construction in 1883 when this photograph was taken. De Mores was quoted in 1886 as saying that the plant would process 100 to 150 steers per day. However, the plant never reached this capacity for sustained periods and failed for a number of reasons, not the least of which was the preference for corn-fed beef by consumers. The plant burned to the ground on March 17, 1907. (Courtesy of the State Historical Society of North Dakota B0485.)

The completed packing plant was a sprawling facility, occupying a large area immediately west of today's Theodore Roosevelt National Park Visitor Center at Medora. The most visible remnant of the packing plant today is the large brick stack or chimney, which can be seen jutting into the sky on the western outskirts of Medora. The plant was built at a cost of $250,000. The site is on the National Register of Historic Places. (Courtesy of the State Historical Society of North Dakota B0356.)

A number of individuals, most of whom appear to be employees of the Northern Pacific Refrigerator Car Company, pose for the camera. The packing plant was only one of a number of the Marquis de Mores's failed enterprises, but undoubtedly the most significant one. (Courtesy of the National Park Service.)

This early view of the packing plant location with surviving brick stack and the de Mores chateau in the background is very similar to what can be seen from the bluff overlooking Medora today. The grounds surrounding the old chimney are now managed as a state historical park under the auspices of the state historical society. (Photograph by Paul Lebo; courtesy of the Leppart collection.)

The Medora to Deadwood, South Dakota, stage line was another quickly established de Mores enterprise started in 1884 to capture the burgeoning freight business to the Black Hills gold mines. For a time in 1883, Dickinson and Medora fiercely vied for the freight business. The venture failed when the freight and passenger traffic never reached the point where the business could survive. Deadwood, one of the four coaches that were used in the venture, is now on display at the Chateau de Mores Interpretive Center near Medora. (Courtesy of the National Park Service.)

The Marquis de Mores left a lasting legacy at Medora, despite the fact that his many enterprises failed. During the years 1883 to 1885, the Medora town site hummed with the din of hammers, saws, and other activities associated with building construction. In December 1884, A. T. Packard, editor of the *Badlands Cowboy* newspaper at Medora, reported that "Medora boasted of a population of 146 men, 39 women, 66 children, and 100 transients." Many of these individuals left Medora after the failure of the packing plant. Medora can now boast of the many tourists that visit the small community during the summer months. (Photograph by W. H. DeGraff; courtesy of Wally Owen, Indergaard family collection.)

Eight

AREA RANCHES

I had studied a lot about men and things before I saw you fellows, but it was only
when I came out here that I began to know anything or to measure men right.

—Theodore Roosevelt

The Custer Trail Ranch is one of the more notable ranches in the Little Missouri Badlands. The ranch was founded in 1881 by the Eaton brothers, Howard, Will, and Alden, who traveled to the area from Pennsylvania. It became the first dude ranch in the United States after many invited guests began paying for the privilege of spending time in the badlands. The Eatons later moved the dude ranch operation to Wolf, Wyoming, near Sheridan, and began guiding guests to the Bighorn Mountains and Yellowstone National Park. An extensive hiking trail in Yellowstone National Park is named the Howard Eaton Trail. (Courtesy of the State Historical Society of North Dakota B0492.)

Howard Eaton was the founder of the Custer Trail Ranch located approximately four miles south of Medora. He also operated another ranch north of Medora which bordered Theodore Roosevelt's Elkhorn Ranch. Eaton was also one of a handful of individuals who were instrumental in supplementing the bison herd in Yellowstone National Park with bison he obtained from the Pablo/Allard herd being held in Montana's Flathead Valley. By the late 1800s, the Yellowstone wild bison herd had been reduced to less than thirty individuals. (Photograph by Trevor McClurg; courtesy of the Leppart collection.)

Custer Trail Ranch, near Medora, N. Dak.

The Custer Trail Ranch headquarters was built on or near the campsite of the ill-fated Terry-Custer Expedition (1876 Dakota column of the Great Sioux War) to the Little Bighorn River in Montana. A butte located east of the ranch buildings was named Picket Butte for the pickets who maintained surveillance for hostile Native Americans. (Courtesy of the Leppart collection.)

The first child born on the Custer Trail Ranch was Paul Lebo. The ranch was later owned by Bill McCarty, the well-known Medora area cowboy and rancher who helped bring cattle herds over what later became historic trails from Texas to North Dakota. The frame structures are outbuildings on the Custer Trail Ranch. The Custer Trail continued as a working ranch for many years. Later the Badlands Lutheran Bible Camp operated facilities there for a number of years. A golf course has been developed on a portion of the ranch recently. (Courtesy of the Leppart collection.)

Captive pronghorn antelope were kept on the Custer Trail Ranch as a guest novelty. The Eaton Brothers also kept young bison and deer for the entertainment of their guests. For a time, Howard Eaton was engaged in an auxiliary business selling some wildlife species for stocking in eastern parks. (Courtesy of the Leppart collection.)

A horse has been "hog tied" in this early cabinet card view taken at the Custer Trail Ranch. It was occasionally necessary to break horses to ride at all of the Little Missouri ranch headquarters. (Courtesy of the Leppart collection.)

Jack Snyder rides a bronc at the Custer Trail Ranch. Visitors would have occasionally been treated to normal ranching activities such as the branding of cattle and the breaking or gentling of horses. (Courtesy of the Leppart collection.)

Chuck wagon scenes would have been a common sight during roundups or other occasions experienced by Theodore Roosevelt, Marquis de Mores, and guests at the Custer Trail Ranch. The chuck wagons were much like a mobile mess hall equipped with a ranch cook. (Courtesy of the Leppart collection.)

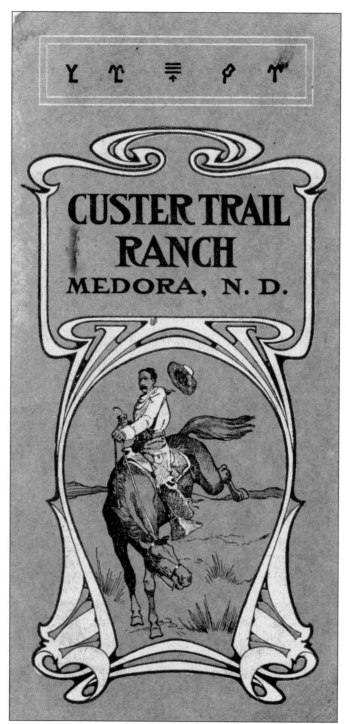

This is the cover of a rare Custer Trail promotional booklet published by the Custer Trail Ranch Company about 1900. Very few promotional items associated with either the Custer Trail or Peaceful Valley Ranches have survived to the present day. This booklet was discovered at a garage sale in Dickinson. (Courtesy of the Leppart collection.)

Initial Rock is a historic landmark located a few miles east of the Custer Trail Ranch on Davis Creek. Two individuals, W. C. Williams and F. Neely, were with the Dakota column during the Sioux campaign of 1876, and carved their names in a sandstone rock near their encampment. Neither individual died at the Battle of the Little Bighorn. (Photograph by North Dakota Tourism Department; courtesy of the Leppart collection.)

"Peaceful Valley Ranch"
Medora N. D.

The Peaceful Valley Ranch headquarters is now located within the south unit of Theodore Roosevelt National Park. The ranch was used by the Civilian Conservation Corps (CCC) at the time the organization was overseeing work crews in the area in the 1930s and early 1940s. The primary building was used as park headquarters in the late 1940s and early 1950s, prior to the construction of new headquarters buildings at Medora. It has also been used as a horse rental and riding facility for decades. The ranch headquarters was placed on the National Register of Historic Places in 1994. (Courtesy of the Leppart collection.)

Peaceful Valley Horses Crossing Little Missouri River.
Medora, N.D.

B.C.Brown.
N.P.Ry.

A band of domestic horses crosses the Little Missouri River at the Peaceful Valley Ranch. This early photograph represents the essence of what ranching in the badlands is all about. (Photograph by B. C. Brown; courtesy of Wally Owen, Indergaard family collection.)

PEACEFUL VALLEY
RANCH - MEDORA, NORTH DAKOTA.

IN THE HEART OF THE WONDERFUL
BAD LANDS OF DAKOTA

PETRIFIED STUMP, 12 FT. IN DIAMETER,
ON CLAY PEDESTAL

Just a Homey Place for Those Who Love the Great
West As God Made It. An Old Time Cow Ranch,
Where We Have Accommodations for a Limited
Number of Guests.

These promotional pamphlets prepared for the Peaceful Valley Ranch were used to entice potential visitors to the ranch. Carl Olson, one of the early owners of the ranch, was also an enthusiastic supporter of the national park concept in the badlands to commemorate Theodore Roosevelt's ranching days. (Courtesy of Wally Owen, Indergaard family collection.)

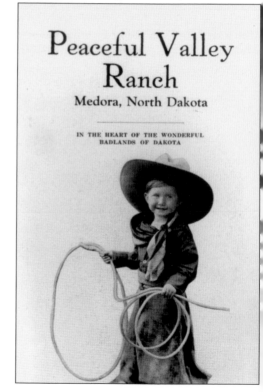

Peaceful Valley
Ranch
Medora, North Dakota

IN THE HEART OF THE WONDERFUL
BADLANDS OF DAKOTA

Branding at the Peaceful Valley Ranch was an annual event. Neighbors from surrounding ranches helped at ranch brandings. (Below, photograph by L. Osborn; both photographs courtesy of the Leppart collection.)

BRANDING CATTLE AT A BADLAND RANCH   L. OSBORN DICKINSON, N.D.

The old Cornell ranch house was also known as the D. K. "Deacon" Wade, and Abe and Clara Collis ranch headquarters. This photograph was taken during the summer of 1970. Theodore Roosevelt had lunch and visited here briefly with Wade and his wife while on a cattle roundup in 1885. The initial construction of this ranch house was begun in 1884 by the LeMoyne Cattle Company of Pennsylvania. D. K. Wade was the company ranch manager. The large L-shaped house was added onto in later years. This structure also became the homestead headquarters of Lulu Cornell. It was one of the earliest ranch structures built along the Little Missouri River bottoms. (Photograph by Gary Leppart; courtesy of the Leppart collection.)

The Cornell ranch house carried a mantle of winter snow when this photograph was taken February 18, 1961. The original roofing material consisted of dirt overlaying several layers of tar paper, which was supported by split cottonwood logs. A wooden frame roof was later added above the dirt roof. The Cornell family cats sometimes enjoyed life between the two roofs. This structure was standing well into the last half of the 20th century. It has since collapsed. Electricity did not come to this structure until 1960. (Photograph by Dick Maeder; courtesy of the National Park Service.)

Ralph Hubbard, Medora naturalist and Native American expert, dozes in the shade in this view of the Cornell place in September 1970. This ranch was also known as the Teepee Bottom Ranch, named for an old Native American wickiup structure that was located south of the ranch house. (Photograph by Gary Leppart; courtesy of the Leppart collection.)

Horses stand in a corral to the south of the Cornell Ranch house in this early view. The house was probably only a few years old. Note the dirt roof. The ranch was probably managed by D. K. "Deacon" Wade at the time the photograph was taken. The juniper snubbing post in the center of this corral was still present in the 1980s. The rest of the old corral had long since vanished. (Courtesy of the Leppart collection.)

Cattle have been brought in from the range in this early view of the Cornell Ranch headquarters. The ranch may have been managed by Abe Collis at the time this photograph was taken. (Courtesy of the Leppart collection.)

Badlands roads in the Medora area were quite primitive and could not always be traveled during wet weather or when deep snow was present. The number of improved roads changed dramatically as oil fields were developed both north and south of Medora during the latter half of the 20th century. During winters with deep snow, travel between ranches and to Medora often took place by driving on the ice of the Little Missouri River. Modern telephone service did not come to some parts of the Little Missouri badlands until the 1960s. (Courtesy of the Leppart collection.)

These two views of the Logging Camp Ranch south of Medora may have been taken by the same photographer. Note the pine trees in the foreground of both images. Pine trees are not common in the badlands near Medora. Most pine stands are located farther south in Slope County. A small grove of ponderosa pine can be seen approximately one mile east of Medora on the south side of Interstate Highway 94. (Courtesy of the Leppart collection.)

Branding activity is a popular subject that appears frequently in early ranch photography. This is probably due to the fact that neighbors helped neighbors during these times and capturing images of helpful friends was desirable. The bottom image is of Louie Pelissier a popular area rancher and rodeo pickup rider. Pelissier was well known throughout western North Dakota and eastern Montana. This image was used on the cover of the June 1948, issue of *North Dakota Outdoors Magazine*. (Below, photograph by Ken Piper; both photographs courtesy of the Leppart collection.)

The presence of lignite coal in the badlands was an important factor to ranchers and residents of Medora. The coal seams were mined largely by pick and shovel with the use of some explosives and provided heat for ranch houses and residences in Medora. Cottonwood logs and old juniper posts were also used for fuel. In the early 1900s, there were several coal mines on the outskirts of Medora. In the photograph to the left, Conrad "Dutch" Ziegler is shown working in the Nichols coal mine in a rare double exposure. (Left, courtesy of the Leppart photograph collection; below, courtesy of Wally Owen, Indergaard family collection.)

The Reid place was located downstream, or north of Theodore Roosevelt's Elkhorn Ranch. This view was believed to have been taken in 1894. (Courtesy of the National Park Service.)

Many of the early ranch structures along the Little Missouri River bottomlands were constructed of cottonwood logs. Where pine was present, that species was used. The Elkhorn Ranch buildings occupied by Theodore Roosevelt were built of locally obtained cottonwood logs. The Maltese Cross cabin was constructed of pine logs cut for railroad ties and floated down the Little Missouri River. The Robert Hanson (HZ) Ranch building as seen here was probably constructed of pine. (Courtesy of the Leppart collection.)

A number of early photographs portray mock hunting and gunfight scenes. This mock gunfight took place on the TIX Ranch which was located approximately 22 miles south of Medora. (Photograph by Radcliff Denniston; courtesy of George and Sydney Hegge.)

A group of Medora-area locals, including Dan Connell (left), are seen relaxing after a Sunday afternoon of boxing. Note the boxing glove on the unidentified man who is third from left. It was also a good afternoon for the Grain Belt Beer Company. This photograph was taken on the TIX Ranch. (Photograph by Radcliff Denniston; courtesy of George and Sydney Hegge.)

A unique gathering of elderly Medora residents was captured in this image. Pictured, from left to right, are H. F. Roberts, J. J. "Jakey" Tomamichel, Ben Bird, T. F. Roberts, W. M. "Badlands Bill" McCarty, B. T. "Barney" Connell, George "Shy" Osterhaut, John F. Reily, J. C. "Chris" Rasmussen, W. W. "Six Shooter Slim" Kunkel, and Paul Lebo (sitting). This image was taken in front of the old Joe Ferris store in Medora on March 31, 1948. (Photograph by George Grant; courtesy of the National Park Service.)

The Connell children, like most youngsters raised in the badlands, practically grew up on horseback. The TIX Ranch house is visible in the background. (Courtesy of the Leppart collection.)

Five Medora area residents pose for a rare studio portrait. From left to right are (first row) Willis King, Eugene "Chi" Otto, and Fred Otto; (second row) unidentified and Harry V. Johnston. The photographer and date are unknown. (Courtesy of the Leppart collection.)

Tom Mix became a very popular early cowboy film star and performer at the 101 Ranch near Bliss, Oklahoma. He also appeared in numerous Wild West shows, and other venues in the United States, Canada, and Europe. Mix spent a short period of time in the Medora area while staying at the Con Short Ranch northwest of town. He married Olive E. Stokes in Medora on January 10, 1909. (Courtesy of Wally Owen, Indergaard family collection.)

This image and others taken at the same time have been reproduced a number of times. The image was created in 1888. The photograph is of the owner of the Little Missouri Horse Ranch and ranch workers. The ranch was located on Deep Creek in Slope County. A. C. Huidekoper, the wealthy owner of this large ranch, is marked with an X. Huidekoper raised large herds of well-bred, imported horses. The Little Missouri Horse Company Ranch, or "HT" as it was known, became one of the largest ranches in western Dakota Territory. Huidekoper, like the Eaton brothers, came to the badlands from Pennsylvania. It almost appears as if the goat has grown an antler in this photograph. (Photograph by T. W. Ingersoll; courtesy of the National Park Service.)

Cowboys rarely pose for studio portraits, but these Medora-area gentlemen did. From left to right are (first row) Henry Peterson (a well-known bronc rider), Ed Dietz, and Henry Nelson; (second row) J. C. "Chris" Rasmussen, Byron Connell, and Jay Brown. (Courtesy of the Leppart collection.)

Wolves were considered a menace to local livestock during the 19th and early 20th centuries. They were often shot on sight. The last wolf known to have been shot in the North Dakota Badlands was killed by Dan Connell in March 1919. The animal had followed the Connell children home from school and had been seen near the ranch buildings the night before it was killed. According to Sid Connell, son of Dan Connell, the wolf was tracked for about two hours. It was shot after Connell surprised it sleeping at a location west of the Little Missouri River, approximately 20 miles south of Medora. (Above, courtesy of the Leppart photograph collection; right, courtesy of George and Sydney Hegge.)

Nine wolf pups were dug from their den in western North Dakota as evidenced in this image from a real-photo postcard dated August 24, 1907. The pups were probably less than two weeks old since their eyes had not yet opened. (Courtesy of the Leppart collection.)

Coyotes, the smaller cousin of the gray wolf, still frequent the North Dakota Badlands. These pups were dug from their den beneath a rock outcropping near Hebron, North Dakota. (Photograph by G. C. Slack and Company; courtesy of the Leppart collection.)

Nine

THE CIVILIAN CONSERVATION CORPS

*If it had not been for what I learned during those years I spent here in North Dakota,
I never in the world would have been President of the United States.*

—Theodore Roosevelt

The Civilian Conservation Corps (CCC) had three camps in the badlands between 1934 and 1941. The CCC was born of the great depression of the 1930s. Its primary purposes were to relieve the unemployment among youth and conserve some of the nation's natural resources. This is company camp No. 2772, located near the juncture of Jones Creek and the Little Missouri River in what is now the south unit of Theodore Roosevelt National Park. This camp closed in November 1941. (Courtesy of the National Park Service.)

The CCC employed about three million young men in the course of the national program's nine-year life span. Enrollees received valuable work experience, training, and education that prepared them for work later in life. The National Park Service provided funding and expertise for the CCC work done in the badlands. (Photograph by Ed Frigen; courtesy of the National Park Service.)

A combined camp of companies No. 2771 and No. 2772 are seen in this view in what became the north unit of Theodore Roosevelt National Park. Camp No. 2772 moved to an area that later became a portion of the south unit. The CCC workers had a significant impact on the early development of the lands which were to be included in Theodore Roosevelt National Park. The CCC also improved other area historic sites, including the de Mores chateau and packing plant. (Photograph by Jerry Orf; courtesy of the National Park Service.)

Ten

THEODORE ROOSEVELT NATIONAL PARK

*America's national parks will ultimately contribute more to the moral strength
of the nation than all the law libraries in the land.*

—James Bryce, British ambassador to the United States, 1907–1913

The dedication celebrating the establishment of the south unit of Theodore Roosevelt National
Memorial Park on June 4, 1949, drew thousands of spectators, many of whom are not visible in
this photograph. The dedication ceremonies were held on sloping ground overlooking Painted
Canyon. (Courtesy of the National Park Service.)

Promotional efforts to establish a park in the badlands to commemorate Theodore Roosevelt's ranching days began shortly after his death in 1919. Dignitaries who were brought to the area to promote the park idea are seen viewing the badlands the "proper way" according to the caption provided by Shy's Store in Medora (above). (Courtesy of the Leppart collection.)

Only a portion of the hundreds of automobiles moving towards the park dedication ceremonies are seen in this view. The photograph shows vehicles turning right into the east park entrance. Dedication events were held along the park road in addition to the primary dedication site overlooking Painted Canyon. (Photograph by George Grant; courtesy of the National Park Service.)

Workers are seen installing the stone work for a park entrance sign in the top photograph. An iron worker, who may be local artist Einar Olstad, is seen putting the finishing touches to a park entrance sign in the bottom photograph. Today, there are a little more than 70,000 acres contained within the three units of the national park. (Courtesy of the National Park Service.)

Badlands scenes typical of the topography now found within the national park were obtained by a number of early photographers, but few did a better job than Paul Lebo. The top photograph was probably taken along the eastern edge of the badlands. As early as the late 1870s, individuals working for the Northern Pacific Railroad promoted the idea of changing the name of the Little Missouri Badlands to Pyramid Park. The railroad was interested in promoting settlement along its route and felt that the Pyramid Park name created a more favorable impression of the region. The name continued to appear at sporadic intervals on postcards, maps, books, and other publications well into the 20th century. (Above, photograph by Paul Lebo; both photographs courtesy of the Leppart collection.)

Nature's Statue of "Sakakawea"
"the Bird Woman"
Badlands near Medora, N.D.
© 1926 by Paul W. Lebo

Despite the fact that photographer Paul Lebo of Medora was disabled when afflicted with polio, he was able to travel throughout the badlands with his photographic equipment and obtain many striking images. A number of Lebo's landscape images are scenes in today's south unit of Theodore Roosevelt National Park. (Photographs by Paul Lebo; courtesy of the Leppart collection.)

The Jars of Ali Baba
Medora, N.D.
Lebo photo

Images of Painted Canyon represent some of the most striking views of the badlands greeting travelers coming from the east. This terrain is within the south unit of the park. The landscape is high in scenic values and low in human footprints. Very few visitors hike into this portion of the park. French trappers called the Little Missouri Badlands "les mauvaises terres a traverser," which when translated means "bad lands to travel through." Sioux Indians called the area the "place where the hills look at each other." (Courtesy of the Leppart collection.)

A visitor views the Little Missouri River from a high point in the Wind Canyon area. A pair of golden eagles nested on these cliffs for many years until their nest slid from its ledge and fell into the Little Missouri River. (Photograph by Vernon W. Erickson; courtesy of the Leppart collection.)

Large petrified logs, tree stumps, log fragments, and leaf impressions are found in a number of places throughout the badlands, including the park. A number of petrified stumps, logs, and wood fragments are visible from the loop road in the south unit. All paleontological and archaeological resources are protected from removal or damage within the park. (Courtesy of the National Park Service.)

The teepee-shaped stick structures found in secluded and usually heavily wooded areas of the badlands are known by a variety of descriptive terms including wickiup, tipi, war lodge, and conical lodge structure. Area archaeologists commonly accept the conical lodge terminology. These structures were temporary shelters used by Native American war or hunting parties. The Hidatsa also used them as part of eagle capturing activities. A few structures continue to exist in secluded areas of the park and elsewhere in the badlands. (Photograph by Osborn, Dickinson; courtesy of Wally Owen, Indergaard family collection.)

Horseback riding is part of the badlands heritage. Hiking and horseback trails have been established in the north and south units of the park, and hikers and trail riders make extensive use of them. The lengthy Maah Daah Hey Trail parallels the Little Missouri River and connects the south and north units of the park. (Courtesy of the Leppart collection.)

The River Bend Overlook Shelter in the north unit was constructed by CCC workers. The north unit contains more deeply eroded and rugged badlands terrain than does the south unit and offers more of a challenge to hikers. The north unit is located 15 miles south of Watford City and is adjacent to U.S. Highway 85. (Courtesy of the National Park Service.)

Longhorn steers were introduced to the north unit to commemorate the Long X Trail, an early historic cattle drive route that traverses a portion of the park. Longhorn cattle are also representative of some livestock stocked on the open ranges during Theodore Roosevelt's ranching days. Watford City, Medora, and Dickinson were home to a number of the early cattle drovers. (Courtesy of the National Park Service.)

In 1956, the North Dakota Game and Fish Department began transplanting the subspecies California bighorn sheep in the North Dakota Badlands. On January 15, 1959, bighorn sheep were reintroduced in the south unit of the park. Most of these animals disappeared, probably as a result of disease. In January 1996, 19 bighorn sheep were introduced into the north unit where wild free-roaming sheep can be seen today. (Photograph by Gary Leppart; courtesy of the Leppart collection.)

Rocky Mountain elk were reintroduced to the south unit of the park in 1985. The transplanted elk came from Wind Cave National Park in South Dakota and were so successful that within eight years, excess animals were gathered and removed from the park. (Photograph by Gary Leppart; courtesy of the Leppart collection.)

Bison, which were once native to the entire region, were reintroduced in the North and South units of the park. The first transplant was in 1956 when 29 bison were transported from Fort Niobrara National Wildlife Refuge in Nebraska, and released in the south unit. In 1962, 20 bison were moved from the south unit to the north unit. Enthusiastic spectators have gathered on the roadway to watch the release. The National Park Service conducts periodic roundups to keep bison herds within management limits. (Courtesy of the National Park Service.)

Wild horses roam throughout the south unit of the park. The horses are the offspring of escaped or feral animals, which have roamed portions of the badlands since the time of Theodore Roosevelt and the Marquis de Mores. The herd numbers are kept to an optimum 60 to 90 head. This photograph is of an early roundup conducted in the 1950s. The structures in the background are at Peaceful Valley Ranch. (Photograph by Leo Lalonde; courtesy of the National Park Service.)

BIBLIOGRAPHY

Brooks, Chester L., and Mattison, Ray H. *Theodore Roosevelt and the Dakota Badlands.* Washington, D.C.: National Park Service, 1958.

Crawford, Lewis F. *The Medora-Deadwood Stage Line.* Bismarck, ND: Capital Book Company, 1925.

—————. *Ranching Days in Dakota.* Baltimore, MD: Wirth Brothers, 1950.

Hagedorn, Hermann. *Roosevelt in the Badlands.* Boston: Houghton Mifflin Company, 1921.

Hagen, Olaf T., and Mattison, Ray H. *Pyramid Park, Where Roosevelt Came to Hunt.* Bismarck, ND: The State Historical Society of North Dakota, 1952.

Jenkinson, Clay S. *Theodore Roosevelt in the Dakota Badlands, An Historical Guide.* Dickinson, ND: Dickinson State University, 2006.

Lang, Lincoln. A. *Ranching with Roosevelt.* Philadelphia: J. P. Lippincott Company, 1926.

Morris, Edmund. *The Rise of Theodore Roosevelt.* New York: Ballantine Books, 1979.

Putnam, Carleton. *Theodore Roosevelt: The Formative Years.* New York: Charles Scribner's Sons, 1958.

Roosevelt, Theodore. *Hunting Trips of a Ranchman.* New York: G. P. Putnam's Sons, 1885.

—————. *Ranch Life and the Hunting Trail.* New York: The Century Company, 1907.

—————. *Theodore Roosevelt: An Autobiography.* New York: Charles Scribner's Sons, 1921.

Sewall, William Wingate. *Bill Sewall's Story of T.R.* New York: Harper and Brothers, 1919.

Tweton, D. Jerome. *The Marquis De Mores, Dakota Capitalist, French Nationalist.* Fargo, ND: The North Dakota Institute for Regional Studies, 1972.

Vivian, James F. *The Romance of My Life. Theodore Roosevelt's Speeches in Dakota.* Medora, ND: Theodore Roosevelt Medora Foundation, 1989.

www.arcadiapublishing.com

Discover books about the town where you grew up, the cities where your friends and families live, the town where your parents met, or even that retirement spot you've been dreaming about. Our Web site provides history lovers with exclusive deals, advanced notification about new titles, e-mail alerts of author events, and much more.

Find Your Place in History.